NUMBER 355

# THE ENGLISH
# EXPERIENCE

ITS RECORD IN EARLY PRINTED BOOKS
PUBLISHED IN FACSIMILE

# THE DECAYES OF
# THE CATHEDRAL CHURCH
# OF ST. PAUL

LONDON 1631

DA CAPO PRESS
THEATRVM ORBIS TERRARVM LTD.
AMSTERDAM 1971 NEW YORK

Published in 1971 by
Theatrum Orbis Terrarum Ltd.,
O.Z. Voorburgwal 85, Amsterdam

&

Da Capo Press
- a division of Plenum Publishing Corporation -
227 West 17th Street, New York, 10011
Printed in the Netherlands
ISBN 90 221 0355 2

1583289

# HIS
# MAIESTIES
## COMMISSION
giuing power to enquire of
the Decayes of the Cathedral
*Church of* St. PAVL *in*
LONDON, and for the re-
pairing of the same.

## LONDON
Printed by *Robert Barker*, Printer to the Kings
most Excellent MAIESTIE: and by the Assignes
of *Iohn Bill.* Anno Dom. 1631.

DIEV · ET · MON · DROIT

# HIS
# MAIESTIES
## COMMISSION.

HARLES
*by the grace of*
GOD *King of*
England, Scot-
land, France, &
Ireland, Defen-
*der of the Faith,* &c.

*To Our truſtie and welbeloned*
A 3 *Sir*

*Sir* ROBERT DVCIE, *Baro-*
*net, Lord* Maior *of the City of*
London, *and to the Lord Maior*
*of the* said *Citie for the time*
*being.*

To the most Reuerend Father
in God, Our right trustie and right
welbeloued Counsellor, GEORGE,
Lord Archbishop of Canterbury, Primate of all England, and
Metropolitane, and to the Lord
Archbishop of Canterbury for the
time being.

To Our right trustie and right
welbeloued Counsellor, THOMAS
Lord COVENTRIE, Lord Kee-
per

per *of the great Seale of* England ; *and to the Lord Chancellor*
*of* England, *and Lord Keeper of*
*the Great Seale of* England *for*
*the time being.*

To *the most Reuerend Fa-*
*ther in* GOD, *Our right trustie*
*and welbeloued Counsellor,* SA-
MVEL, *Lord Archbishop of*
Yorke, *Primate of* England, *and*
*Metropolitane, and to the Lord*
*Archbishop of* Yorke *for the time*
*being.*

To *Our right trustie and right*
*welbeloued Counsellor,* RICHARD,
*Lord* WESTON, *Lord high*
Trea-

*Treasurer of* England, *and to the* Lord high *Treasurer of* England *for the time being.*

*To Our right trustie and right welbeloued Cousins & Counsellors,* HENRY *Earle of* Manchester, *Lord Keeper of Our Priuy Seale, and to the Lord Keeper of Our Priuie Seale for the time being.*

ROBERT *Earle of* Lindsey, *Lord high Chamberlaine of* England; *and to the Lord high Chamberlaine of* England *for the time being.*

THOMAS *Earle of* Arundel

del *and* Surrey, *Earle Marſhal of* England ; *and to the Earle Marſhal of* England *for the time being.*

PHILIP *Earle of* Pembroke *and* Mountgomery, *Lord Cham*berlaine *of Our Houſʰold, and to the Lord Chamberlaine of Our Houſhold for the time being.*

*To Our right truſtie and right welbeloued Couſins and Counſellors,* THEOPHILVS *Earle of* Suffolke, *Lord Warden of the* Cinque-Ports.

EDVVARD *Earle of* Dorſet,
B        *Lord*

*Lord Chamberlaine to our dearest
Consort the Queene.*

WILLIAM *Earle of* Salisbury.

WILLIAM *Earle of* Exeter.

IAMES *Earle of* Carlile.

HENRY *Earle of* Holland,

HENRY *Earle of* Danby.

EDVVARD *Viscount* Wimbledon.

DVDLEY *Viscount* Dorchester

ſter, one of Our principall Secretaries of State ; and to Our principall
Secretarie of State for the time
being.

THOMAS *Viſcount* VVent-
worth, *Lord ʼPreſident of Our
Councell eſtabliſhed in the North.*

*And* HENRY *Viſcount*
Faulkland.

*To the right Reuerend Fathers
in God Our right truſtie and wel-
beloued Counſellors,* WILLIAM
*Lord Eiſhop of London,* and
RICHARD *Lord Biſhop of*
VVincheſter; *and to the Biſhops*

*of* London *and* Winchester *for the time being.*

*To the right Reuerend Fathers in* God, IOHN *Lord Bishop of* Ely, *and* FRANCIS *Lord Bishop of* Norwich,

*To Our right trustie and welbe-loued Councellours,* EDVVARD *Lord* Newburgh *Chancellour of Our Duchie of* Lancaster; *and to the Chancellour of the Duchie of* Lancaster *for the time being.*

*Sir* THOMAS EDMVNDS, *Knight, Treasurer of Our Hou-shold; and to the Treasurer of Our Houshold*

*Houshold for the time being.*

*Sir* HENRY FANE, *Knight,*
*Comptroller of Our Houshold; and*
*to the Comptroller of Our Houshold*
*for the time being.*

*Sir* THOMAS IERMIN,
*Knight, Vice-Chamberleine of*
*Our Houshold; and to the Vice-*
*chamberleine of Our Houshold for*
*the time being.*

*Sir* IOHN COKE, *Knight,*
*one of Our principall Secretaries of*
*State; and to Our principall Se-*
*cretaries of State for the time*
*being.*

*Sir*

Sir FRANCIS COTTING-
TON, *Knight, Chancellor and Vn-*
*der-treasurer of Our Exchequer;*
*and to the Chancellour and Vnder-*
*treasurer of the Exchequer for the*
*time being.*

Sir ROBERT NAVNTON,
*Knight, Master of Our Court*
*of Wards and Liueries; and to the*
*Master of the Court of Wards and*
*Liueries for the time being.*

*And Sir* IVLIVS CÆSAR,
*Knight, Master of the Rolles; and*
*to the Master of the Rolles for the*
*time being.*

To

*To Our* truftie and welbelo-ued, *Sir* NICHOLAS HYDE, *Knight,* chiefe Juftice of the Pleas before Vs to bee holden ; and the chiefe Iuftice of the Pleas before Vs to bee holden for the time being.

*Sir* THOMAS RICHARD-SON, *Knight,* chiefe Iuftice of Our Court of Common Pleas ; and to the Chiefe Iuftice of Our Court of Common Pleas for the time being.

*Sir* HENEAGE FINCH, *Knight,* Recorder of Our City of London ; and to the Recorder of the Citie of London for the time being.                    *Sir*

*Sir* ROBERT HEATH,
*Knight, Our Attourney generall:
And Sir* RICHARD SHELTON,
*Knight, Our Sollicitor Generall;
and to Our Attourney and Sollicitor
generall for the time being.*

*And Sir* HENRY MARTIN,
*Knight, Judge of the Prerogatiue
Court of* Canterbury; *and to the
Judge of the Prerogatiue Court
of* Canterbury *for the time
being.*

*To Our trustie and welbeloued,
Sir* WILLIAM BVLSTROOD,
*Knight, Sir* THOMAS MID-
DLETON, *Knight, Aldermen
of*

*of the said Citie of* London.

*Sir* HENRY SPILLER,
*Knight.*

*Sir* ROBERT PYE, *Knight.*

*Sir* HVGH HAMERSLEY,
*Knight*, *Alderman of the said
Citie of* London.

*Sir* IAMES CAMBEL, *Knight*,
*Alderman of the said Citie of*
London.

THOMAS WINNIFFE,
*Doctor in Diuinitie, Deane of the
Cathedral Church of Saint* Paul
C                        *in*

*in* London, *or to the* Deane *of the* said Church *for the time being.*

NICHOLAS RAYNTON.

RAPH FREEMAN.

ROVVLAND HEYLIN.

ROBERT PARKHVRST.

RICHARD FENN.

*Sir* MAVRICE ABBOT, *Knight.*

HENRY GARVVAY, *and* WILLIAM ACTON *Knight and*

*and Baronet*, *Aldermen of Our
said Citie of* London.

I O H N  M O V N T F O R D,
*Doctor in Diuinitie.*

H E N R Y  K I N G, *Doctor in
Diuinitie*, *Residentiaries of the Cathedral Church of* S$^t$. Paul *aforesaid*; *and to the Residentiaries of
the said Church for the time being.*

*To Our trustie and welbeloued,*
F R A N C I S  W I N D E B A N K E
*Esquire, one of the Clerkes of Our
Signet.*

W I L L I A M  N O Y, *Esquire.*
  C 2        WILLIAM

WILLIAM HACKVVEL,
*Esquire.*

EDVVARD WYMARKE,
*Esquire:*

*And* ROBERT BATEMAN,
*Esquire, Chamberleine of Our City
of* London *; and to the Chamberleine of the said Citie for the time
being, Greeting.*

WEE *haue taken in-
to Our serious and
Princely considerati-
on , the present state
and great Decayes of the Cathedral Church of* St. Paul *in* London*,*

don, *the same being the goodliest*
*Monument, and most eminent*
*Church of our whole Dominions,*
*and a principall ornament of that*
*our Royall Citie, the Imperiall Seat*
*and Chamber of this Our King-*
*dome, whither by reason of the*
*neere Residence of Our Selfe and*
*the chiefe and principall Officers*
*of Our State and Courts of Iustice,*
*there is continuall confluence both*
*of Our owne Subiects, and of Am-*
*bassadours from forreine Princes,*
*and other Strangers.*

  *In respect whereof, and of Our*
*zeale to Gods glory, and his Diuine*
*Worship and Seruice in that goodly*
*Church, and for the honour of Our*
*gouerne-*

gouernement, Wee haue an earneſt
deſire and purpoſe to prouide by all
poſſible meanes for the repayring
and vpholding of that munificent
ſtructure, and reſtoring the ſame ( as
time and meanes ſhall by Gods bleſ-
ſing giue aſſiſtance ) vnto the ancient beauty and glory of it, which
by lying ſo many yeeres neglected
is now become a worke of neceſſitie
to be vndertaken.

And calling to minde the pious
care and gracious intention of Our
moſt deare and Royall Father
King IAMES, to begin and ſet
forward that Honorable and great
Worke, who granted a Commiſſion
vnder the Great Seale of England

land *to many of your selues Our
now Commiſsioners, and some o-
thers, with sundry good directi-
ons to that purpose, Wee haue re-
solued by Gods aſsistance, in pursu-
ance thereof, to proceed to the act-
ing and executing of that which
by his late* MAIESTIES *decease
was interrupted and out of the light
taken from that Commiſsion, and
thoſe beginnings, to put the same
into the most probable way for the
reall and substantiall effecting of
Our Princely hope and earnest deſire therein.*

*And duely weighing with our
selues that as this chargeable Fabricke and goodly Pyle of building
could*

could not in the first founding ther-
of but require both many yeeres of
time, and large supplies of publike
charitie, and yeerely contributions
to sustaine the charge thereof: So
the substantiall repaire and adorning of it intended by Us, is not to
be effected out of any Rents, Reuenues or Possessions, which haue
beene heretofore pretended to haue
beene giuen, limited or appointed
for the maintaining or repairing of
the Fabricke of the said Church,
concerning which, great and diligent inquirie was made vpon the
said former Commission, but with
little successe, neither will the same
proue a worke suddenly to bee effected,

*fetled, but will require both a great
ftock of money, and Materials
to begin the worke, and a conftant,
yeerely fupply (and that for fome
good continuance of time) to bring
it to an end. Wee therefore well
knowing that the fafe keeping of the
moneyes and materials which fhall
be prouided for fo great a Worke,
and the faithfull and frugall difpo-
fing thereof for the good vfe intended and no other, are the firft and
principall things to bee fetled therein, to giue both Our Selfe and Our
louing Subiects affurance of good
fucceffe, Doe hereby declare, and
Our will and pleafure is, that all moneyes of all forts to bee raifed, had,*

D         or

or recouered for the *Worke* aforefaid, *fhall bee brought* and paid
into the *Chamber* of London, *as*
the fitteft and fafeft Cheft where-
into the fame can be put, to be there
furely kept and difpofed apart by
it felfe for the vfe aforefaid, and
to bee iffued out from time to time
for the faid vfe, in fuch manner
as is hereafter by thefe prefents
mentioned.

And therefore Wee doe hereby
will and require all and euery per-
fon and perfons that haue or fhall
haue the Collection or bringing in
of any fumme or fummes of money
to the purpofe aforefaid, that they
pay the fame duely to the Chamber

ber of London; and also that the
Lord Maior, Aldermen, Chamberleine, and other Officers of the
same Citie to whom the same doth
or shall appertaine, doe from time
to time receiue the same to bee there
kept and disposed of as aforesaid,
and that they giue acquittances and
discharges, to the parties of whom
they receiue the same.

And Our further will and pleasure is, that the materials and prouisions which already are, or shall
from time to time bee brought in
for that worke, shall be kept in such
Storeyards, Houses and Places,
and by such Officers as shall bee
appointed for that purpose, accor-

D 2        ding

ding to the true intent of these
Presents: And not to bee issued
out, spent or disposed of, but onely
for the said publique vse of repairing the Church aforesaid, according to such Warrants and Di-
rections as shall from time to time
bee giuen for the same by such as
shalbe thereunto authorised by these
Presents.

And whereas Wee vnderstand,
that the right reuerend Father in
God, GEORGE late Bishop of
London, did in his life time, at
his proper charge, prouide and lay
ready in or neere the Churchyard
of the said Cathedrall Church, good
store of large Purbeck-stones, for
and

and towards the reparations of the
said Church.

And that albeit by vertue of the
said Commission of our said deare
father, diligent search and enquiry
was made vpon view of the Euidences pertaining to the Bishop of
London, and Deane and Chapter
of Pauls, yet it could not bee made
appeare, that any of the possessions
of the said Bishop and Deane
and Chapter, were giuen for the re-
payre of the said Church ; Ne-
uerthelesse, you Our said Counsellor
the now Lord Bishop of London,
haue freely offered out of the de-
cayed Reuenues of that Sea, to
allow the summe of one hundred

Pounds

Pounds by the yeere, whiles you
shall continue in it, towards the said
Worke.

And Wee doubt not, but that
the said Deane and Chapter, will
of their owne good dispositions to so
pious a worke, contribute thereunto, in a more franke and liberall
manner, then vpon the strictest en-
quirie, they are or can be liable to
doe. Our will and pleasure is, that
as well the said prouisions of stones
shall bee presently taken into the
charge of such Officers, as shall bee
appointed in that behalfe, as par-
cell of the Stocke of Materialls,
prouided for the good worke aforesaid. And also that the said one
hundred

*hundred pounds* per annum, *ſhall yeerely vpon the ſeuenth day of October,* (*or on the morrow after, when the ſeuenth day falls out to bee Sunday*) *bee du ly payed into the Chamber of the ſaid Citie of* London , *together with ſuch yeerely ſummes, as the ſaid Deane and Chapter ſhall or wil contribute from time to time, for the vſe aforeſaid, according to Our pleaſure generally before declared, for all moneys and Materialls, to be brought into that purpoſe.*

*And becauſe Wee are very confident, that many others of Our Nobilitie and louing Subiects, will bee ready to follow the good examples afore-*

aforesaid, by voluntary and liberall
contribution, for raising a present
Stocke to begin the worke withall,
Our will and pleasure is, and Wee
doe hereby giue and grant vnto you
Our said right welbeloued Counsellor WILLIAM Lord Bishop
of London, and to the Bishop of
that Sea for the time being, full
power and authoritie, to prouide
and keepe a Booke or Register
( like vnto that Booke which was
made and kept in Our said deare
Fathers time to that purpose)
wherein to take the seuerall Sub-
scriptions of all such of Our Nobilitie, Bishops, Iudges, Sergeants
and Counsellors at Law, Officers,
and

and others of qualitie and abilitie,
as shall willingly contribute to the
said worke, for such seueral summes
as they shall in their Christian charitie freely bestow in that behalfe,
and to cause the moneys so subscri-
bed, for to bee payd into the Chamber of London, as aforesaid, accordingly.

And Our further will and pleasure is, and We doe hereby straight-
ly charge and command the Iudges
of the prerogatiue Courts of both
Prouinces, and the Vicars generall, and other Officials of the seuerall Bishoprickes of this Our
Kingdome and Dominion of
VVales, that from hencefoorth
they

they take speciall care out of such
moneys as shall from time to time
fall into their power vpon the de-
ceases of any Our louing Subiects
dying intestate (to bee distributed
Pios vsus) to remember in that
some conuenient proportion thereof
bee assigned and set apart towards
the supply of the said Worke, whereof the Bishops in their seuerall
Diocesses are to take notice re-
spectiuely, and to make Certificate
thereof to the Bishop of London
for the time being, at the end of e-
uery sixe moneths, and withall to
cause the moneys so reserued, to be
sent vp and payd into the Chamber of London, within that time
accordingly.                    And

And for a further supply of this great and chargeable Worke, which will neceſſarily require a generall and liberall Contribution of all Our able Subiects of the Kingdome to bee made by Our Letters patents to that purpoſe, but the ſame to bee drawen in a more ſpeciall maner then ordinary Protections are wont to bee, according to the extraordinary nature of this caſe ; Our will and pleaſure is, and Wee doe hereby ordaine and appoint, that all ſuch Letters patents in nature of Protections, as ſhall from time to time bee aduiſed and found needfull for the aduancing of the ſaid

E 2    Worke,

Worke, *shall bee made and granted vnder Our great Seale of England to that purpose, in such maner and by such Warrant and Direction, as hereafter in and by these Presents is declared.*

*And to that end that an honourable and orderly course may bee taken for all thinges needfull for this weightie businesse, as well for taking an exact Suruey of the particular decayes of the said Church, and calculating the charge thereof, as for discouering and finding out of all such Legacies, Gifts, Bequests, Summes of Money, and other Profits, as haue beene heretofore, giuen or intended for*

the

the maintenance, repayring or a-
dorning the said Church, as also for
the safe and orderly collecting and
bringing in of all such Moneys,
as shall from time to time bee collected, had, raised, or recouered for
that publique vse, and of all Materials thereunto belonging, and
the well disposing, issuing, and em-
ploying thereof, and orderly ac-
compting for the same.

Wee reposing speciall trust and
confidence in your approued Wise-
domes, sincerities, and dexterities,
haue made speciall choice of you, to
be Our Commissioners, to see Our
Will and pleasure herein declared,
duely effected, and put into reall

E 3　　　Ex-

*Execution, not doubting, but by the Honourable care and iudgments of you the Lords of Our Priuie Councell, and the diligence and faithfulneſſe of you the Lord Biſhop of London, and the Deane and Reſidentiaries of that Cathedrall Church, and the truſt and forwardneſſe of you the Lord Maior, Aldermen and Chamberlaine of Our ſaid City of London, this great Worke ſhall by the helpe of many hands ioyned together in one way of integritie, be brought to a happy and glorious Concluſion.*

*Know ye therefore that We haue aſſigned and appointed you to bee Our Commiſſioners, and Wee doe*

*by*

*by these Presents giue full Power
and Authoritie to you or any sixe
or more of you ( whereof three to
bee of Our Priuy Councell, and
the Bishop of London to bee al-
wayes one ) from time to time either by your owne view and Suruey, or by the aide and assistance of
such skilfull workemen or other persons, as by you or any such sixe
or more of you shall bee thought
meete, to search, discouer, try, and
finde the true state of the said
Church, and the particular Decayes thereof, as well in the
Steeple as in the Body and other
parts of the said Church, either in the Foundation, or in the
Walls,*

Walls, Pillars or Couerings thereof, in Stone worke, Timber-worke,
Lead, Iron, Glasse or otherwise
howsoeuer. And what sorts and
quantities of Stone, Timber and o-
ther materials the substantiall repaire of the same will require, and
what the charge thereof will by probable estimate from time to time a-
mount vnto, and what part of the
Worke is fittest to bee first vndertaken, and of most necessitie, and
in what time the same may bee
done, and what other parts to bee
next set vpon in the times and
yeeres subsequent, with the charge
of each yeeres worke, and all other
circumstances, whereby you may be
                                    informed

*informed of the natures and sorts of the seuerall Decayes, and the meanes, time and charge of the repaire of the same.*

*And further Wee doe giue vnto you, or to any such sixe or more of you, as is aforesaid, full Power and Authoritie, as well by view of any Records, Bookes, Rolles, Euidences or Writings, or by examination of any witnesse or witnesses, or others vpon Oath or without Oath, or by any other wayes or meanes, to enquire, examine, discouer and finde out, what Legacies, Gifts, Bequests or summes of money haue beene heretofore giuen, raised, collected, leuied, or recei-*

F        *ued*

ued for or towards the Reparations or adorning of the said Church
and not imployed already to that
purpose, and in whose hands the
the same now are, and all other circumstances touching the same. And
to aduise and consider by what
meanes the same may bee brought
in, and paid to the Chamber of our
Citie of London, according to
Our Direction before specified, and
to put the said wayes and meanes
into due and speedy execution.

And Wee doe also hereby giue
vnto you Our said Commissioners,
or to any such sixe or more of you,
as is aforesaid, full Power and
Authoritie from time to time to
consult,

consult, aduise and agree of such
forme and formes of Letters Patents to bee granted in the nature
of protections for publique Collections to be made within Our said
Realme of England and Dominion of Wales, of the charities
of Our louing and well-disposed
Subiects towards the Worke aforesaid, to bee collected and brought
into the Chamber of Our said Citie, reciting therein so much of the
Premisses as shall bee found needfull, and putting therein such o-
ther necessarie Clauses as you shall
conceiue most likely to aduance the
Collections and Contributions to be
made thereupon, which said Let-

F 2                    ters

ters Patents of Protection so to be
aduised and agreed vpon vnder the
hands of such sixe or more of you, as
is aforesaid, We will and command
you Our said Keeper of Our Great
Seale now being, & the Lord Chancellor of England, and the Lord
Keeper of Our great Seale of England for the time being, to passe vnder Our great Seale of England,
without any further or other Warrant from Us to bee procured or ob-
tained in that behalfe : And these
presents shall bee vnto you, and
them, and euery of them, a sufficient Warrant and Discharge for
the same.

And whereas We well know that
in

*in the managing of so great a Worke*
*there will necessarily fall out*
*many other particulars to bee set-*
*led and agreed vpon, for the order-*
*ly and frugall gouerning and gui-*
*ding of the Receipt and Issuing of*
*the moneys and Materials for*
*the same, and the exact keeping of*
*the accompts of both; Our will and*
*pleasure is, and Wee doe hereby*
*giue full power and authority vnto*
*you, or to such sixe or more of you,*
*as is aforesaid, vpon conference*
*together, to agree vpon, and appoint*
*what Surueyours, Paymasters,*
*Clarkes and other Officers shall*
*be employed, aswell in the keeping*
*of the stores and Materials, as in*

F 3 *doing*

*doing any other thing concerning
the premises, and to minister vnto
all, or any of them, whom you or any
such six or more of you shall thinke
fit, such oath or oathes, for the due
performance of the seuerall imploi-
ments, charges and trusts to them
or any of them to be committed, as
to you, or any such six or more of you
shall be thought reasonable and conuenient; and to consider of, aduise
and agree, in what manner the
bookes and accounts both for the
moneys to be brought into the said
Chamber of London, and the materials and prouisions to be brought
into the Stores, shall be from time to
time kept and controlled, audited,*

*trans-*

tranſcribed and certified from time
time ; And to make and ſet
downe particuler orders and inſtru-
ſtions, aſwell for the iſſuing of the
monyes from the Chamber of
London, to the Paymaſters, who
are to be imployed in the payment
of moneyes for wages, materials,
prouiſions, cariages, or otherwiſe
concerning the ſaid workes; as alſo
for each ſeuerall mans charge and
imployment therein, and to aduiſe,
treat and conſider of all other
things, wayes and meanes for
the aduancement and furtherance
of his great and emnient worke,be-
ing of ſo much conſequence for preuenting the diſhonour which by
the

the neglect of so ancient a *Mo-*
*nument* might fall vpon Vs , and
the whole *Nation* , and to put the
same waies and meanes into speedy
and due execution; for the doing of
all which, these Presents shall bee
your sufficient warrant and discharge .

And We doe further hereby giue
full power and authority vnto you,
or any such Sixe or more of you, as
is aforesaid, to consult, aduise and
consider of meet orders, ordinances
and constitutions, for the better pre-
seruation and maintenance of the
said Cathedrall Church in time to
come; and for the suppressing and
preuenting of all present and future
annoy-

annoyances, purprestures and en-
crochments, which doe or shall tend
to the damage, hurt, blemishing or
disgrace of the said Church: And
the same orders, ordinances, and
constitutions being reduced into
writing, to present vnto Vs, to the
end that the same being by Vs per-
used and considered of, may receiue
Our royall approbation and allow-
ance, with such further order from
Vs for the strengthning of the
same, by Our owne Royall signa-
ture, or otherwise as Wee shall find
meet.

And Wee doe hereby giue full
power and authority vnto you, or
to any such sixe or more of you, as

G                                        is

is aforesaid, to cause all and euery
person and persons, whom you shall
thinke good, to bring and shew before you, or any such sixe or more
of you, either vpon oath, or without oath, all and singular such Records, Bookes, Euidences, Accompts, and other Notes and
Writings, as you or any such sixe or
more of you shall thinke fit to bee
produced; whereby the truth in the
premisses may the better and more
plainely bee found out and discoue-
red. And for your more ease and
expedition in the execution of this
Our Commission : Our Will and
Pleasure is, aud Wee doe hereby
Charge and Command, that all
                                    such

ſuch Surueyors, Actuaries, Regiſters, Officers and Miniſters whatſoeuer, which you or any ſuch fixe, or more of you ſhall thinke fit and require, ſhall be readie and attendant vpon you, or any ſuch ſix or more of you, for the doing and performing of any thing neceſſary to bee done in the execution of this our Commiſſion.

And to the intent that your doings and proceedings in the premiſſes may be the more firme and inuiolable, and may remaine in perpetuall memory for the good of the ſaid Church in time to come; Our will and pleaſure is that you, or any ſuch Sixe or more of you,

as

as is aforeſaid, ſhall make certificate thereof into our Court of
Chancery, that the ſame may there
remaine of Record.

And laſtly Our pleaſure is
that this our Preſent Commiſſion, ſhall continue in force:
and Wee doe hereby authoriſe
you our ſaid Commiſſioners, or a-
ny ſuch Sixe or more of you, as
is aforeſaid, to proceed in the
execution thereof, and of all and
euery matter and thing therein
contained, from time to time,
and as often as you, or any ſuch
Sixe or more of you ſhall thinke
conuenient: albeit the ſame Com-
miſ-

miſsion bee not from time to time continued by Adiourne-ment.

In witneſſe whereof, Wee haue cau-ſed theſe Our Letters to bee made Patents : Witneſſe Our ſelfe at Canbury the tenth day of Aprill in the ſeuenth yeere of our Reigne.

G3

¶ Imprinted at London
by ROBERT BARKER,
Printer to the KINGS moſt
Excellent MAIETIE:
and by the Aſſignes of
IOHN BILL.

M.DC.XXXI.